This Way About

This Way About

KATHERINE HOOVER

THIS WAY ABOUT

iUniverse books may be ordered through booksellers or by contacting:

iUniverse
1663 Liberty Drive
Bloomington, IN 47403
www.iuniverse.com
1-800-Authors (1-800-288-4677)

ISBN: 978-1-4917-6037-6 (sc)
ISBN: 978-1-4917-6036-9 (e)

Library of Congress Control Number: 2015902068

Print information available on the last page.

iUniverse rev. date: 05/19/2015

Contents

Foreword

Katherine Hoover is best known to us consumers of the arts as a musician, a splendid flutist and a composer who writes works of lasting merit. Now she reveals to us different but related talents as a poet.

High-level artists who practice more than one art form have long been with us. To cite just a few examples, poets William Blake and Vachel Lindsay illustrated their own poetry with fine work. Paul Klee, Ansel Adams, and Theodore Roethke were serious students of classical piano playing. And think of all the song writers who write both words and music. These are two very different arts, yet people like Cole Porter, Joni Mitchell, and Stephen Sondheim could have been great successes either as lyricists or composers alone. (Remember, Sondheim's first hit was *West Side Story,* for which he wrote only the lyrics.)

Hoover's poetry seems to me closely related to her music. We often speak of poetry as musical when, in addition to the meaning of the words, their sound has its own interest. Sometimes, we even enjoy hearing the work of a great poet in a language we don't understand. Hoover's poetry is full of music: rhythmic patterns, assonances, internal and end rhymes, and so on. Reading the poems out loud reveals their sonic pleasure and prompts the reader to a musical reading, inflection arising from the text. The collection ends with some poems that have music as their subjects, but the music is present throughout.

These poems frequently are deeply heartfelt. They are also wonderfully varied, from the overtly emotional quality of "Circles" to the vehemently polemical "Looking for Love in All the Wrong Places." "Nocturne" is pure music both in subject and in sound. Frequently, I discover lines and images that I want to copy down and eventually steal, like "sometimes the phone rings / too loud" (from "Living with Sorrow") and "I wonder / what it is that you give / to children, to lovers / if you don't give them / part of yourself / to keep?" (from "Detachment").

In this collection, Katherine Hoover has given us parts of herself to keep.

—Leslie Gerber, music critic and author of the recently published poetry collection *Lies of the Poets*

Vaguely Philosophical

It is not the road that leads into
but also (or only) about.
It is the fish that flies over the water.
I circle backward: perhaps
out springs right of way.
Who is to say
that backward is not
where forward will go?
Let someone else decide;
I abstain,
knowing simply myself
that this way about
is only (or also) mine.

Handiwork

This quiet pool
changes hour to hour,
day to day.
The sun hits
a plume of sea grass
and tall stalks with
crinkled leaves.
A carp, fire orange
with white fins, darts
about, while another,
larger, with bright epaulets
and pale, translucent tail
glides slowly
through the water.
White lilies open and close.
A fountain molds its tune
to the breeze; a frog croaks.
All shifts, evolves, beauty
flowing like clouds
in a summer sky.

People have made this and
tend its drifting harmony.

At the beginning
of this present war
as bombs pelted Baghdad,
there was a photograph
in the *New York Times.*
One minisecond, framed,
static. A hospital corridor,
two young doctors in

scrubs, stricken, shamed,
standing by a long pile
of small green bags
stacked against the wall:
children's bodies.
I suppose it has all been cleaned up,
corpses burned or buried, the
blood scrubbed and bleached.

This, too, people have made.

Prism

By the porch light,
spidery lines
radiate
silver tracery
in harmonic waves,
an equation of
elegance.
Drops on the web
split the light
into flashes of
color.
The weaver sits
quietly
at the center
of this ephemeral
cathedral,
spins with
immaculate persistence
to eat, to live.
Tomorrow,
she begins anew,
casting out
of herself
to infinity.

Year's End

Ghosts
of things
that didn't happen
things that did
pieces written
or forfeited
friendships
that were only smiles
smiles that blossomed
for a while, at least
crises that struck and
passed, leaving marks unseen
Ghosts
that mean everything
and nothing
crowd past
my private sight
in customary
disorder

Three women on a bus
babushka, glasses, heavy feet
all in stockings
on a bitter cold day.
Incalculable patience sits
on their unadorned faces
      Sudden hot darkness
      in a blacked-out city
      crowds milling
      restlessly
      car horns, and lighted
      candles in the stairwell

The handsome young lawyer
accepting easily
four months of my wages
with his pipe and smile
and superb
tailoring
Running in the park
electric exhilaration
In a brisk wind
sweatshirts, ruddy cheeks and
brotherhood
with the fast and slow
      The hospital, a loved one
      cruelly thin
      clutching his ill-fitting white
      garment as if it were
      the last shred
      of his dignity
A small dinner party
wine and easy laughter
strange musings
from an uncomfortable husband
bob like rowboats
on a pitching sea

    Is this
the sum, the total?
Why no, there's
      the kind friend who
      brought me home in a taxi
        the midnight call

sun on a piece of sculpture
       the creeping boredom of
       a waiting room

Ghosts
are not containable
there are always more
the past
is piecemeal
continuous only in
fiction
Ghosts
are what we are given
to live with.
Is this why

Is this why
we crave sequence so
ordering our days
our work, our homes
structuring machines
to create infinite
order, sequence
beyond comprehension

beyond comprehension
the mind returns
to its more or less
comfortable
Ghosts
       a jumble of fresh country
       colors at a farmers' market

a smashed car window
one blossom on a
delicate plant
Sequence
is subtle
it is not neat
Ghosts
random, willful,
insistent are the only
clues

Ardmore Station, February

Gray above slate branches,
black trunks,
pasty green below.
Here and there, old brick
casts pallid brown
against the gray,
and a tangle of bush,
matted, colorless.
Dirty rust rails
lead never away,
only stare.
Nearby, stolid under
pigeons' probing,
stone buildings
whose windows
face arid streets
watch bleary-eyed
a few scattered parcels
of human traffic.

Valor—'80s Style

By God we do it well.
It is the essence, the mark
of our time.

Violence, death we accept
with resolution.

Streets reek of carnage
and pain, the corruption
of money stares at us.

What bravura we display—
each morning a proud face
greets the world.

Yesterday the Holocaust.
Tomorrow the Bomb.

Still we are polite
(Have a nice day).
We congratulate ourselves
on our fortitude, our
grace under fire.

Faith and love have little
hold on us (figments of
need, of imagination).

Beauty is exterior
decorating, gilded
figures on the lid of
Pandora's box.

All we have left
is the depth of our
courage (wherever it
may come from).

By God we do it well.

The Widow

I as the land
am shrouded in white;
the land hides
under the white
starched cover
of a nun.

My widow's weeds
of weeping,
flowing cloaks
of cold coal,
cover as the white
covers a nun's soul.

Chastity is a penance,
a white snow
pressed upon
the world's soul.

Strange Tears

Strange tears, shed for love newly lost
though lately gained. A calf's cry, sigh
of mourning wind as I see flown
a sudden summer's day of the heart
with ponderous beauty and foreign, forgotten
promise of nothing to come.
Short shrift for much grieving, but still
his strength sang sweetly in my thighs, his eyes
were firelit, words gentle as the arching night,
which fled so fast, leaving lightly
its broken-winged words of hope. I flew,
and again aloft on the words' wings I rose
till they shattered, and hope clattered,
cracked on the hard ground.

Suddenly Spring

Suddenly the trees are budding pink.
Suddenly they're green.
Suddenly the park invites
... no jackets required.
Suddenly daffodils and
beach towels bloom,
runners and cyclists
shed layers,
skin seeks the sun.
Toddlers romp in the playground
where a backpack hangs
from a hippo's ear.
Birds cluck and chatter,
white blossoms spread their
fragrance, and mica
winks back at the sun.
Soon, all the bare branches
will be tucked away
with coats and sweaters.

Sentinel

In the yard stands
a tall tree, a fir—
oh, taller than that, even
taller than that ...
it's hard to see a bird
on its crown.
Long, curving branches brush
the roof of our small house.

Sometimes at night
I slip into the trunk
and rise through the wood,
rise with the sap
pulsing up, up to the crest
and out into a hundred limbs
to thousands of stretching hands
and a million green fingers
that lift and ripple
in the breeze.

It is cool and dark
in these great branches.
I feel the nests huddled within
where newborn birds stretch forth
beaks, then wings, and at last
their songs.

By day, I survey my kingdom
across yards, roads, and fields
to the bay and the ocean beyond—
a crow caws from my peak,
provoking a raucous squabble;

squirrels dart and chase;
blue jays whistle; and
woodpeckers drill,
looking for lunch.
Small bothers, these, for the
privilege of the seasons:
snow on my branches,
sudden showers, bracing winds,
the sun, the moon,
and the sweetness of early spring.

My roots run deep,
deep into the ground;
my reach is magnificent.
Here under my spreading wings,
I cradle the hearts
of my wild creatures
and of those in the
small house below.

Scrub

If I grow bitterly
like a gnarled and stunted tree,
bearing harshly of my youth
puckered fruit that sears the mouth—
if I make of my drawn boughs
an inhospitable house
out of which I never pry
toward the water and the sky,
inside which I stand and hide
and hear the day go by outside—
it is that a mind too strong
bent my back when I was young;
it is that I fear the rain
lest it blister me again.

There Was No Love

"There was no love for you
in that house," she said.
A continent away, in our thirties,
she tore open the locked box
of my childhood. Shock
silenced me, then electric
flashes leapt about wildly,
smashing into walls,
leaving gaping holes
in the box.

That was years ago.
Now it is tired fact:
there was no room
in the heart of a woman
trapped in an alien existence
and a man obsessed
with her distress—
no room for others.
There was food, a bed,
an angry older child.
As I grew, more doors
slammed shut, and I dreamt
of the day I would leave
forever. I didn't know
I had locked the box within;
distortions twisted my life
till it exploded
that day in London.

Was harm done? Yes.
Who is to blame? No one.
When a violent storm is over,
we drag away the big branches,
rake the lawn, throw away the
broken pots, and replace
what cannot be fixed. It takes
time, but what is left
is what is strong.

The Flowers

The flowers ... you don't
know how much they mean ...
nor do I. I cannot
comprehend them. Every
color blooms here: orange
and amber; shades of blue,
magenta, crimson, white,
and green, of course; palm
and iris leaves. Myriad
shapes of buds, petals,
stamens, stems, branches
blend in a massive,
glowing beauty.
         The Japanese
study one or two blossoms
at a time to catch an
essence, a distillation
of line or texture ...
         I am
bewitched by this utterly
unbounded profusion of
color, form, and love.
It speaks eloquently of
the richness we give
each other and the
fragments we understand.

Hell and Heaven

Forget the imps and pitchforks,
the flames and pointy tails.
Hell is a personal place
we visit in secret,
The Very Worst Things
You Have Ever Done
confessed endlessly to a
phantom therapy group,
frozen in shock, hands
clapped over open mouths
as the prison doors swing wide.

Heaven, on the other hand, is
harps, clouds, pearly robes,
silly St. Peter jokes.
Nothing personal about it.
Good weather, I presume.
Once, when pressed, I pictured
a large swimming pool
with no chlorine; chocolate;
and lots of snow peas.
Also, I would like
to make beautiful music
with very little
practicing.

The Courage of Success

A well-known author
was interviewed
many years ago.
Her novels were violent
and well reviewed
in the best publications
by known critics.
She held a chair
at a prestigious
university.
The interviewer asked
had she ever considered
a happy ending?
She said yes,
she had wanted to try it
once,
so she wrote a
short story
under a pseudonym.

Nocturne

It is night on the fifth floor,

sitting in the dark,

watching tangles of branches

drawn by streetlights

on my wall.

Here in this room,

I work, I ponder.

I pull together threads

of days and weave

a strange, lumpy fabric,

plaids and paisleys intertwined

and a few loose strings.

Hope drops by to say

the moon is out, somewhere

above the buildings.

I offer a cup of tea.

She smiles and moves on,

and I sleep.

Upper West Side Pilgrimages

Today
I come
to this building
to be pummeled and kneaded,
relieved of the indignities
of age
as years ago
I went
to the building
next door
to be kissed and caressed,
relieved of the urgencies
of youth.

Looking for Love in All the Wrong Places

One day, I
set out to look
for a place to
gather myself,
to be quietly
encouraged
in my attempts to
live with love.
Sometimes the road is
full of stones, shadows
haunt us, Death
knocks nearby, fear
waits in a corner.

So I put on my jacket and
walked.

Here is St. Barnabas.
The doors are open.
I sit and watch
men in rich robes
moving about this
beautiful place.
Women are welcome
to sit and listen
but not to serve except
by withdrawing to a
cell, giving alms,
or bearing young in
a prescribed manner.
I leave.

A synagogue. The main doors
are locked—safety first,
of course—but there is a
small side door.
The sanctuary is calm,
well-kept, and light with
all that is needed for
quiet reflection.
I settle in. Then it
comes to me: ten men
are needed for any ritual
or blessing, and that
prayer to thank God for
being born a man.
I cannot rest here.

I pass by a mosque with
my head uncovered:
I do not choose
to hide myself.

Here is a simple
church, Methodist
or Unitarian—they have
women ministers.
I enter and relax into a
comfortable, cushioned pew.
Here at last, a sense of
openness ... yet theirs
is a bearded God
who reigns with his
God-like son born of a

Woman who was not
a woman but a girl
untouched, too young
for the experience, the
knowledge, the power
of womanhood. She
is no goddess: she is
an accessory.

Is there no place
for me to seek the light,
to be encouraged to live
and give with the power
rightfully earned by
creating, suffering,
nurturing, learning?
Who dares to say
we are less for this?

Let us make a place
for women to be
so honored,
and let it be inclusive.
If men come, they will be
welcomed as equals to
those who bore them
but no more.

The Moon

Round, silver white,
she spread her light
through bare branches
and leafless vines
along the wall,
etching bricks
on the porch
where I sat watching.
The air was charged,
electric; vibrations
transformed,
whispered ...
Reach, she said.
Stretch out your hands
and pull me
into your heart,
for you reflect me
as I reflect the sun:
this is what
we are.
It swept through me
as a wave moves through
a fisherman's net,
leaving fragments
caught glittering
in its wake,
bearing witness
like luminescence
in the sea.

Heddles

In an African room
at the Metropolitan Museum,
there are beaded crowns,
tall wooden sculptures,
high-domed black masks,
and small carved heddles.
There are intricate plaques
of heroes and kings
made in brass centuries ago
by a complex
lost wax method,
and there are heddles.
There are thrones and
gold ceremonial staffs,
abstract antelopes,
stylized snakes and
monkeys, and heddles.
At last I ask,
What is a heddle?
Our young friend
whips out a phone
and types it in.
Wi-Fi is weak, she says,
but soon we learn that
it's about weaving:
Set across a loom's top,
heddles hold the
long warp lines straight
as shuttles move across,

creating the bold fabric
of Africa, keeping
the patterns
sharp and strong.

In My Dream

In my dream,
I saw exiles
driven by war
and hunger.

In my dream,
they huddled
in snow on the
edge of being.

Yet in my dream,
they returned
after years
to the place
they had fled,
silent, wary,
to settle again
among old,
familiar stones
and strangers.

In my dream,
their hopes were
fragile, their
faith was frail,
yet the heart
still longs
to love.

Convergence

Bratislava, 1992

On a wide plain,
one great hill
rises to a castle.
Neolithic bones
have been found here;
monarchs once fled here.
A road spirals up
from the city below
past tall houses with
broken shutters,
peeling paint.
The Soviets left only
recently; wrecked concrete
walls litter the plain.

Mist whirls by as I
walk the road to the
castle, now being
restored. All is informal.
People are scarce, and
work is slow on this
gray day. I move
through sparse rooms:
a sword, a cape,
tools, sawdust,
drawings ...
Familiar patterns
catch my eye, designs
painted on barns
where I once lived.

I climb alone to the top,
to a watchtower of six
sides with great glass
windows. As I stand
searching out a view
through the clouds,
a hawk appears.
Motionless, we stop
and watch each other.
Then, like a ball slowly
unwinding, I step
to the next window.
The hawk follows.

And so we begin a
silent, circling vigil
around the tower,
I moving, pausing,
the hawk lifting, gliding,
then perching nearby,
a long, liquid dance.
Here, in the
deepening fog, with
ancient bones and
monarchs, we rise
and swirl, connected
and suspended
in the mist.

Dust

Manhattan, September 21, 2001

The dust is cream colored.
The dust is everywhere.
Here, miles above the
disaster, it sits on
our windowsill.
It has settled
on our hair, our
hands, our minds.
We are hollow
and smothered
as we go about
everyday tasks
on automatic
pilot.

pilots planes
flames smoke
death and more
death
screaming escapes
explosions
heroic acts
and more
death
implosions shown
over and over
stampeding jumping
and more death
twisted steel and
mountains of shredded

debris and
cream-colored dust

Black bars have sprung up
around my heart, my head.
I peer out between them
at a dimmer world.
Everything is
farther away.
Part of me
is filled with
cream-colored dust.
Scrubbing will not
wash it away;
it is embedded.

Candles at the firehouse,
the precinct burn
through our numbness.
They died for us.
Requiescat in pacem.
Rivers of money flow
for survivors, families;
blood banks are
overwhelmed.
We cannot give enough
in our grief.
We gather in halls,
temples, churches
to mourn and honor;
our pride in our own
cannot be assuaged.

With flags and tears
we will endure
whatever is decided
by leaders whose
vision is shadowed,
who must act
though all roads
are dark.

Neighbors, friends,
strangers hug and
hold hands,
shocked into awareness
that we love and
that we must
proclaim it.

In our new room,
a ladder with tools,
books left open
on a table
are as precious
as the freshly laid tile.
A sweater dropped
on a chair is proof
of your presence.
We measure everything
differently now;
we have
what so many
have lost.

LIVING WITH SORROW

Detachment

A psychologist once
told me at a party
that mourning is natural
as long as you don't feel
that you've lost a part
of yourself.
He was a nice man
and sincere in his
statements. His house
was beautiful, his
wife and children
were beautiful, and he
watched them with
devotion.

My friend wasn't beautiful.
He'd been ill for a year
before he left.
We both lived in
apartments and led
separate lives,
which crossed
whenever we could manage.
We had stopped
drawing lines between us
long ago,
and our most precious
possessions
had been exchanged;
but that part of me
he couldn't leave; nor could he
reclaim what I had.

It has nothing to do
with me. My will
is not involved; really
I'd much rather it didn't
happen at all, but at times
the part of him
that is with me
cries out for the rest
painfully,
and sometimes my body
screams for what was
given for safekeeping,
then taken far
away.

Now I wonder
about the psychologist
with his lovely wife,
with his beautiful house
and family.
He seemed well read
and thoughtful, yet
I wonder:
What is it that you give
to children, to lovers
if you don't give them
part of yourself
to keep?

Poems on the Death of a Loved One

I

Joy sits
in a strange place,
for death
has released it.
Caged in suffering
and weariness, it
fell silent, forgotten
under the cloth
of care.
Now in the hush
of death,
the dumb knell
of mourning,
it has slipped its cage
and flown.
A narrow note sings
past my sorrow,
a tentative trill—
Time is a bastard
beggar, it says,
Love is king.

II

The rain has done it.
The funeral didn't do it,
nor the necessities of
daily bread, the quiet calls
to friends.
Death came as a bell toll,
cavernous and low, vibrating
through tenuous days; its
resonance moved with me
beyond sleeplessness and
involuntary fast.
Rather soon, I seemed to be
working again, various parts
connected, the engine
turning over slowly,
responsibilities reassumed
lists made, digits dialed, lunch,
and occasional laughter ...

Now suddenly on this second day
of gray rain, time has stopped...
The dishes are undone, there are
too many lights on
in this house... I do not want
to move... I watch
the steady drumming on the
pavement, filigree patterns by a
streetlamp, rivulets rushing
past a gutter.

No need to weep—that is all
being taken care of.
There is nothing
I need do. I desire only
to twist into these silent
silver pins,
pulsing against the earth,
streaming toward
gentle fusion.

III

I will never be the same,
not for the death—that
fracture will mend—
but for the life.
Where to begin?
A thousand things—
your dapper bearing, the
slim fingers,
summer walks, swimming
face to face,
a hundred books,
and the laughter,
so much laughter ...
gentle sayings no one
else would understand.

How does one write a love poem
to the dead?
I will never be the same, never again.
Your eyes—never have I known
such eyes.
I see differently
because of those eyes.
The totality of your embrace,
the embrace of a wanderer
home at last.
The trust beyond trust
is an entity beyond separation,
a permanent fixture,

and the music that so deeply
intertwined our lives
remains.

I weep too much. I seem to be afraid
I will forget you, but
you are closer than forgetting.
You are part of all the love
I will ever give.

IV

I have a friend from
another culture
whose husband, dead a year,
came to her again
last week.
He has come several times.
She sees him, feels his arm
around her. She says
he can't stay long, that
they never can.

On Tuesday after
the night of your
faraway death,
I sat numb in my ancient
wooden chair when
suddenly
I was contained
in a womb of
comfort, of wisdom
and a stunning sense
of presence.
How long it was
I don't know; it seemed
a different sort
of time.

My friend's husband tells her
to be easy; he is

at rest, and she did
all she could.

For me there were
no words, no images,
only tracks
across my soul.
You who gave so much
in life brought me this
ultimate gift,
for only the dear dead
can truly release
the living.

Living with Sorrow

Living with sorrow is like
living with anything else
the laundry still gets done and
breakfast comes and goes
each morning
my mailbox is filled
a radio plays next door

certain things I do alone because
memories come so
suddenly
sometimes the phone rings
too loud

the corner market stays open late
you can always pick up
a newspaper there
and every evening
the trains arrive and night
comes on

I read longer before I
turn out the light

What Have I Done

What have I done
with your death?

I've put it in
a battered old suitcase
that I carry
wherever I go.
It weighs a lot
but I always keep it
with me.

What have I done
with your death?

I've made a long cape
with a hood.
I wrap it all around
carefully, so I can
peek out
but nobody will notice.

What have I done
with your death?

I've got it
in a little movie
camera inside.
I play it at night when
I'm alone like a
peepshow, sometimes
even twice.

I wish—

I wish I could
bury it in a garden
under the rich, black earth
and watch the flowers
bloom.

Then maybe I could
pack the cape and
camera in the
suitcase
and leave them
someplace.

Solitaire

One by one, quietly,
deliberately,
she would flick the cards,
deal them out, watch, and
study. Another hand,
again, another ... the game
remained, static, infinite.

It was incredible to me,
her daughter; she never
grabbed an ace or smiled
or swore; the piles
of cards were always neat
and spaced just so.
Not every day, but often,
year after year.

Last week
I found myself
playing solitaire.
I play with some abandon;
I cheat a little now and again,
and the piles spill over
a bit ...
but I recognize
the game.

Weeping Mary

Behind a quiet column
in a cavernous hall
she stands as she has
stood for centuries.
Her wooden cowl flows
to her feet; her shadowed
face inclines; her plain,
strong hands rest on
her robe.

When I first met you,
Mary, you wept for
me, for I was lost.
Years later, I am
found but have lost
others. I come again
to seek your tears,
to entreat your
patient grace.

You have stood forever
silent in cold, stone
rooms. You have seen
violence, pestilence,
famine, wars. You
have lost your son to
the bloody race of man,
and you had no
daughters.

I watch the nodding
figure, so warm, so

elusive. Her spine
is straight, her skirt
falls in perfect
folds. Hers is not the
wail of bereavement, the
cry of a heart pierced
in pain:

Her sad eyes have seen
beyond, where flames
of knowledge are consumed
by the fire of the sun.
In this dim stillness,
gentle Mary weeps in
compassion, as precious
and infinite
as time.

Circles

Bridal wreaths, holly wreaths,
bracelets of bronze and
hammered silver, hoops
and haloes, rings of all
description.

Even space is curved, they say
(though proof is lodged
in straight-edged formulae).

Memories, spun off in time,
whirl in overlapping orbits
and jostle like tops.

Funeral wreaths, laurel wreaths,
chains, collars of brass
and gold, jeweled crowns,
spoked wheels of all
diameters.

Some circles exist only by
inference (rainbows, earrings,
and great spiraling stairways).

Earth has gone once round
the sun since you left it
last green April. I embrace
this year as I once
embraced you.

November Evening

Brahms, wine in crystal,
confetti; autumn frost
intensifies
the warmth indoors.
Children asleep, holidays
around the corner ...
Winter will settle soon
with packed ground, frozen
snow. Alone behind
the hill, I shall
hack out a grave and
bury his death; then
in rooms redolent with
pine and punch
next to a fireplace, in a
new dress, I too will smile
and sing. The children
will bring me presents.

The Waterfall

I walked among the tall pines,
my heart leaden. Into
the heat of afternoon
I wandered, sunk
in bitterness, an intruder
in this quiet place, my feet
dragging, my anger
lashing out at towering
trunks, stately,
oblivious.
The air was still.
A soft rustling
pierced my numbness.
Drawn by the insistent
murmur, I turned and slowly
threaded my way
toward the swelling sound,
jogging as it grew closer,
louder, surging as I
rounded a bend
and looked up into a
tumbling, splashing tide
pelting the rocks,
beating its way
to a churning pool below,
hurling fistfuls of
diamonds at the sun,
its force drawing my force,
calling my anger,
calling my grief,
surrounding my senses
and pulling me forward,

pulling me into
the roar and pounding
pulsing, calling ...
I stumbled in.

I awoke by the pool
to moonlight.
A cool breeze caressed my
shoulders; soft mist
brushed my face.

I lay stunned, drained;
dampness and the sound
of the waterfall enveloped me.
As I lay drenched, dazed,
the roaring water
sang to my bones:

Know me!
I leap in the sun and
rush to the sea.
I glory in strength
and move in rapture,
for I am the blood
of the land.
Storms pelt me
with trees, rocks, mud;
I wash them, tumble and
release them; but I
am myself, powerful
and clear;
I move in freedom.

Why do you let
your griefs possess you?
Do you not laugh in the sun
and love the sea
as much as I?
Do you not celebrate
your strength
and move in rapture?
Open the gates
of your heart
that the flood
of liquid light
may clear the mud
and cleanse your soul.
Claim your glory, and
rise and sing with me.

Alleluia!

AND YOU, MY FRIENDS ...

Emily Sat

*For Emily Dickenson, Georgia O'Keeffe,
Gertrude Stein, & Judy Chicago*

Emily sat alone in her room
and wrote to every one of us,
a questing soul
in a cloistered space
tracing out the days
of her garden, her solitude,
stunning us with her
simplicity.
"I'm nobody," she said.
"Who are you? Are you
nobody too?"

Georgia, famously married,
living among artists, loved
clear light and contrasts.
Once she painted a barn
with heavy, muted tones.
The artists said, "Look! She's
finally learned to use color
well." (Like us, they meant.)
Georgia left the city,
the circle of painters,
the famous photographer
and went to the desert
alone.
There in the sparse brush
and piercing light,
she taught us to see
the single blossom

with its clear, bright colors
and its luminous
feminine mysteries.

Gertrude fled to Paris
with her Alice, where they
didn't fuss about such things,
drove an ambulance in the war,
hosted a notable salon,
invited everyone
who was anyone,
delivered the Word to us
and us to the Word.

Judy Chicago stayed home
and set out dinner plates for
worthy women at a table,
each one a singular wreath
of art and honor.
The table now stretches
around the world.

Where do we find our voices?
In a room, a desert,
in Paris, at a table,
in our hearts, in our desire
to tell the world
what the Word is.
The Word is, the Word is
what the Song is,
the Plate is, the Flower,

the Word is nobody,
the Word is everybody,
the Word is Us,
all of Us.

A Change of Plans

Imagine a world without
Peter Rabbit,
Flopsy, Mopsy,
or Squirrel Nutkin.
It might have been.

Young Beatrix Potter
had an exceptional eye.
She drew constantly,
carefully, and artfully.
She loved the
wildly varied look
of mushrooms, rich
in mysteries of shape,
color, form. As she drew,
she saw intricate
relationships among
lichens, mosses, and the
myriad fungi. She
studied, then wrote up
her conclusions. A
gentleman read her paper
to the learned naturalists
of the honored Linnean Society
(no women allowed).

They said no,
it could not possibly
be true.
Why did you
bring this here?
Waste of time.

Beatrix, discouraged,
abandoned her
mycology studies,
adjourned to a farm
to breed sheep.

A scientist died;
a beloved author
was born.

There she created
wry stories about rabbits,
ducks, farmers, and
exquisite pictures
accurate down to the
tiniest detail,
which have charmed
and enlightened
for a century.

A century
is a long time.
One hundred years
after that meeting,
the learned men
of the Linnean Society
announced
that her theories
were correct and
apologized.

Long Distance

And you, my friend ... we are
an odd pair, truly.
We both alight in
far fields, but you leap
without a net, while I inch
my way cautiously. You mirror
the lightning that rumbles
and flashes in me; I reflect
the cool blue lake so deftly
disguised in you.
Each of us is climbing
a separate slope a thousand
miles distant, loosely roped
by a phone cord.

Valentine

Pick it up
you dropped it there
what is it
it's red and
quivering and
shaped just like a
No no you can't
have it it's mine
I hadn't
noticed it was
missing

Short Order

Well, handsome, I guess it's
not in the stars, but
I'll have
the touch of your suede
vest and the sweep
of your shoulders
to go.

Missing Merlin

These rooms are
full of you, sweet
friend, hidden in
a chair as black as
your lustrous coat
or curled murmuring
in a lap.
Incandescent eyes,
fierce yet quick
to comfort, a
benevolent monarch
of our days,
a gentle Morpheus
of our nights.
Lost or left too
young, bones weak,
yet we persevered
till the day you sat
immobile on our
back step, staring
at a tree, then
suddenly
raced, leapt;
claws dug high
in the trunk,
triumphant,
essential, secure
in our hearts.

Suzanne

In this small house
filled with a lifetime of
far continents, living,
traveling, framed faces
of faded sepia and
grinning infants,
surrounded by weavings,
books, paintings,
her own and others,
Suzanne pauses here,
somewhere between
Peru and France.
Living alone
is warp and weft:
solitude yet freedom
for a restless spirit
whose laughter and tears
bubble over, who welcomes
life with open arms.

Portrait: Norman at Twelve

If I could draw,
I would draw him—
the curve of
his cheek, the
mischievous grin,
an amazing length of leg, pale
and firm,
a boy still,
basking in privilege
of childhood yet
curious, one large
foot planted
timidly
in the future.
Photos tell
his looks at two or ten;
I see him only now—
tousled hair, a
chipped tooth, slim
shoulders that betray
the beginnings of
confidence,
and in his dark blue
eyes, feelings
that most boys try
to hide.

Kathy

Kathy sits
across from me over coffee.
"I can't read," she says,
and her blue eyes
are steady. Smiles
come easily to that face;
they always did.

second row by the window, another pretty singer

It was a lively class:
controversy, constant
dialogue, and strange new
sounds echoing about.
She sat listening.
Sometimes she talked;
she wrote
and sang for us.

Did you hear about Kathy? They've operated on her brain.

Calls to the hospital,
hushed rumors and
reports in the faculty
lunchroom. Little hope.
Silence. A fist
bangs the table.

Very sorry ma'am; only family allowed

Two years ... vague news
of more operations, ominous

predictions.
Bury it. Cover it
over. Life goes on.
The kids here today
never even knew her.

a tape recording ... her voice in my classroom again

In a dim hallway
by the elevator,
hair cropped short
like a boy's,
she calls my name,
half exuberant,
half shy,
slow of speech.
We hug each other
and walk together.

Is it real? Will she disappear again?

She's singing, taking
a lesson now and then.
I write her a note,
begin to see her
in the building.
Then we meet
on the bus. "I admire
you because you do
what you want
by yourself," she says.

O, Kathy, both your parents died before this

> Now she sits
> across from me over coffee,
> talking eagerly of a recital.
> Her hair is longer.
> Her face has grown
> quite beautiful.
> She cannot write, and one side has
> partial feeling.
> She will graduate,
> though she has lost
> much of what she learned.

Someone has written a book about her; they're taking her on tour

> Kathy, I am
> overwhelmed.
> It's not supposed to
> happen like this,
> not today.
> Courage is unfashionable.
> People won't believe
> you. They will stare and
> be unkind.
> It's so much easier
> to pretend
> these things don't happen
> than to let them
> into one's life.
> Can you understand

just how incredible
you are
and how little others know
of their own fortitude?
So few of us are
tested this way.
Even fewer
pass with honors.

Sing, and teach me more than I ever taught you.

Anniversary Song

These years have flown by.
Have we been together
a quarter century?
Our hands meet of their own accord
when we walk, and strangers smile.
Little do they know (or do they?)
how we have built our castle
of faith, of shared excursions
into the realms of belief,
of work, of daily matters
while keeping the arrow
pointed toward its mark,
whatever that turns out to be.
An unlikely couple, it seemed,
yet one in our quest to thrive
singly and together.
I salute us.
I salute you, and me:
we have kept the faith.
May it always be so,
now and forever.
Yours, truly in love,
Katherine

I MADE A QUILT ONCE

Poetry Class

Cut it
cut it down
pare it
strike till there's
nothing
but the core.

But the core
is inedible.

Some Days Are Like That

jostled profundities
awkwardly scrawled
... disgruntled prose
or
reams of verbiage
image profusion
... scannable void

Seminar: Day 1

There is a fishbowl
on this table, empty,
none too clean.
Twelve strangers gather,
begin to talk.
Words begin to drift
toward the bowl; some
slide off and crawl
around the table,
some hang on its edge, and
others settle inside.
I feel an affinity
for this bowl, open,
somewhat dusty from use,
reflecting the light and laughter,
waiting to see
what comes my way
to stay.

Disorderly Construct

You know them.
They stare at you
with the wrong
word in the
right place or
the right word
marooned in
blather.
Can this poem be
saved? Can it be
born again? Or
has the preacher
fled, leaving a
trampled field
littered with
clichés?
That oh-so-
delicious fragment
snickers at you,
sticks out its
tongue.

My Quilt

I made a quilt once.
I took some leaves,
a spider web,
flowers, rain.
I cut them in pieces,
sewed them in strips,
and bound them with
ribbons.

I made a column of clay.
I cut three deep slits
and pulled them together
with patches.
Then I made a cup
inside out,
joined the pieces
side by side,
put handles where
they don't belong.

Doing what
must be done
day after day
is overrated.
Better to run
barefoot, hatless
in a summer shower
chasing metaphors.

Bach: Prelude in C

It's a piece any instrument
can play—a single line,
sweeping down then looping up,
curling about itself.
It was early; the cavernous
stone room was dark,
resonant. Gray mist
covered the lawn outside.
I was working to keep each
note round and full yet part
of a curving line pulling
the phrases forward,
over and over.
Finally, I paused,
gathered my thoughts,
and plunged into that
first declamatory descent:
claiming the space,
notes echoing from
wood and stone, circling
about wrought-iron spirals,
acting, reacting, a part of
the rich harmony.
As the music evolved,
the mist began to rise, leaving
a multitude of sparkling
drops on the grass,
each separate but fused
in a resounding chorus
of sight, of sound
joining and augmenting

the glorious echoing:
the voice of Bach,
illuminating,
transforming.

Music, My Love

Music, my love,
you spoke to me as a child,
watering the desert of my heart;
beckoning with urgency,
you took my soul
for your own.

Music, my love,
you speak to me of
lofty mansions, of
intricate structures,
of richness, of austerity;
of dreams and stories
heroic and intimate.

Music, my love,
you have brought me
to endless gardens of
blossoms, trees,
cactus, and stone;
wherever I look,
you are there.

Music, my love,
you sing out in
cathedrals
built for one
who does not
speak to me
as you do.

Music, my love,

you have taken my hand
in sorrow and led me
from darkness.
You have taught me grace
and forgiveness.

Music, my love,
you whisper to me
of paradise.

Master Teacher

for William Kincaid

"Good!" he said.
"Now mind you,
it wasn't Very Good
or Excellent ...
but it was Good!"
A shock of white hair,
piercing blue eyes,
and a smile
lurking not
so far away.

Though I arrived with
a pedigree, a prize
already won, he
took me back:
simple notes in
simple groups,
over and over,
learning to listen as
never before,
setting up
scaffolding:
a structure
to carry the
weight of
sculpted phrases,
strong bones
to hold the flesh
of living sounds.

He said I must
take careful notes
after each lesson,
but he never asked
to see them:

I did not,
could not
forget.

Studying Syrinx

"Syrinx" is a short piece for solo flute written in 1912 by Claude Debussy about Pan's pursuit of the nymph Syrinx; to save her, the gods turned her into a reed, which was used by Pan to fashion his flute.

We all play it
as students,
a small piece
moving like an
improvisation yet
carefully notated.
Interpretations are
widely divergent,
confusing.
Debussy, they say,
wrote it quickly
backstage somewhere.
Once I heard it played
so the last notes
lingered on and on ... but
when I tried, it was
stilted, like a tail pinned
by a blindfolded child
on the paper donkey.

So I began again,
first with the story
that brought forth such
musical magic, then
testing each sound,
moving, slowing,
increase, decrease,

breathe, listen,
find the shape
that brings life,
that leads to the next
mysterious beauty,
building phrases
like a mosaic.

A long, soft call comes high
from a distant hill, pauses,
then approaches. The sound
comes close; the melody lifts,
then pauses again: he
sees her. A story
unfolds in graceful
twists and turns of
yearning, of desire,
pulling forward, then back
as he whispers, cajoles.
The tempo increases—
she turns away,
he is afire, he reaches, she
whirls swiftly
into a reed, and here,
here is where Pan's
pain is cruelest, and yes,
here is the loudest
marking ... then
the sounds tumble
down, recalling
the hope, the searing

sadness, the sweet
nymph who becomes
his flute, moving
into the last long notes,
stretching, sinking slowly,
softly, into silence.

Acknowledgments

I would like to thank Barbara Goldowski, fine writer and friend, for her suggestions and encouragement; Leslie Gerber, poet and producer, whose help in promoting my work has been essential; and the Omega Poetry Workshop for pushing me forward. I'm grateful also to my artist friends: Lola Stanton, for her drawings, and Bill Stanton, for his cover design. Finally, my deepest thanks to my husband, Richard Goodwin, and son, Norman Schwab for constant patience and care.

Katherine Hoover
Biography

Katherine Hoover was born in West Virginia and grew up in the suburbs of Philadelphia. Following her lifelong love of music, she graduated from the Eastman School of Music with honors. After further study in Philadelphia, she moved to New York, where she taught flute in the Juilliard Preparatory Division and later music theory at the Manhattan School of Music. During this time, she performed widely and began composing music, continuing to write poetry from time to time.

Now best known as a composer, Ms. Hoover established Papagena Press in 1990, which is distributed by Theodore Presser Company. She has won numerous honors, and more than thirty CDs of her work are available. In recent years, she has given more attention to poetry, participating in workshops and readings. Her poem "Dust" (about 9/11) was published in the *Southampton Press.*

Ms. Hoover lives in New York with her husband, Richard Goodwin. Her website is www.katherinehoover.com.

Printed in the United States
By Bookmasters